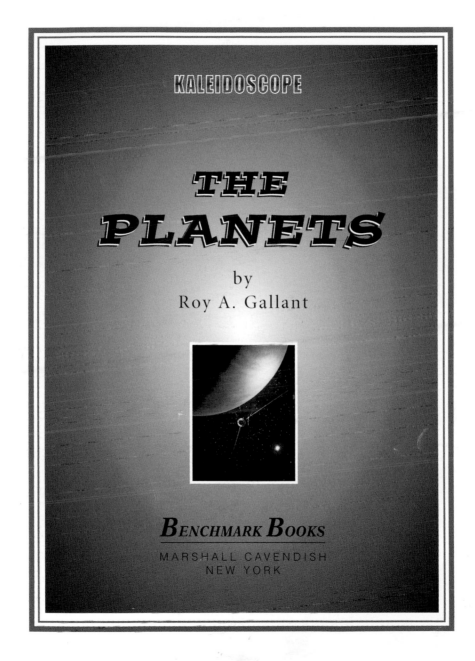

KALEIDOSCOPE

THE PLANETS

by
Roy A. Gallant

BENCHMARK BOOKS

MARSHALL CAVENDISH
NEW YORK

Series consultant:
Dr. Jerry LaSala, Chairman
Department of Physics
University of Southern Maine

Benchmark Books
Marshall Cavendish Corporation
99 White Plains Road
Tarrytown, New York 10591-9001

Library of Congress Cataloging-in-Publication Data
Gallant, Roy A.
The planets / by Roy A. Gallant
    p. cm. — (Kaleidoscope)
Includes bibliographical references and index.
Summary: Describes the nine planets that make up the solar system.
ISBN 0-7614-1033-3
1. Planets—Juvenile literature. [1. Planets. 2. Solar system.] I. Title. II. Kaleidoscope (Tarrytown, N.Y.)
QB602.G35 2001   523.4—dc21   99-047491

Photo research by Candlepants Incorporated

Cover photo: Photo Researchers, Inc./Seth Shostak/Science Photo Library

The photographs in this book are used by permission and through the courtesy of:
Photo Researchers: ©Frank Zullo, 5; © A.S.P./Science Source, 14, 35. ©NASA/Science Source, 17, 28, 36. David A. Hardy/Science Photo Library: 6, 32. JISAS/Lockheed/Science Photo Library: 9. Science Photo Library: 10. U.S. Geological Survey/Science Photo Library: 13, 22. David P. Anderson, SMU/ NASA/Science Photo Library: 18. European Space Agency/Science Photo Library: 21. NASA/Science Photo Library: 25, 31. Science Photo Library: 27. U.S. Geological Survey/Mark Marten: 39. Chris Butler/Science Photo Library: 40, 43.

Printed in Italy

6 5 4 3 2 1

CONTENTS

THE SKY LONG AGO

On a clear night, gaze up into the sky. It will look exactly the way children saw it more than three thousand years ago. Like you, they could count hundreds of lights twinkling against the black sky. These were called the *fixed stars.*

They could also see larger dots, which over several nights seemed to move among the stars. First, the dots would shift one way, then they would seem to stop, back up, and then move forward again. Those large dots were *planets*, or the *wandering stars*, as they were once called. The sky since those ancient days has hardly changed at all. Our understanding of it, though, has changed a lot.

Like the Sun, the stars parade across the sky, rising in the East and setting in the West.

OUR PLACE IN SPACE

It took many centuries before stargazers—or *astronomers*—came to understand what the Sun and planets were made of, and what caused the planets to *orbit*, or move around, the Sun in our part of space known as the *Solar System*.

The planets revolve around the Sun. Their speed is just fast enough to keep them from falling into the Sun.

Today we know that the Sun is a star. It looks much larger and brighter than other stars and feels very hot, simply because it is so close to Earth. The Sun is a huge ball of very hot gases. The main gas is hydrogen, along with some helium. Like other stars, the Sun gives off energy as light and heat. This makes life possible on Earth.

All nine planets of the Solar System circle the Sun. It is as if each planet were tied to the Sun on a long string and swung around and around. But instead of a string, a force called *gravity* holds the planets in their orbits. You can think of gravity as the glue that holds the Universe together.

The Sun's corona, or outer layer. The bright areas are flares, superhot flames shooting out into space.

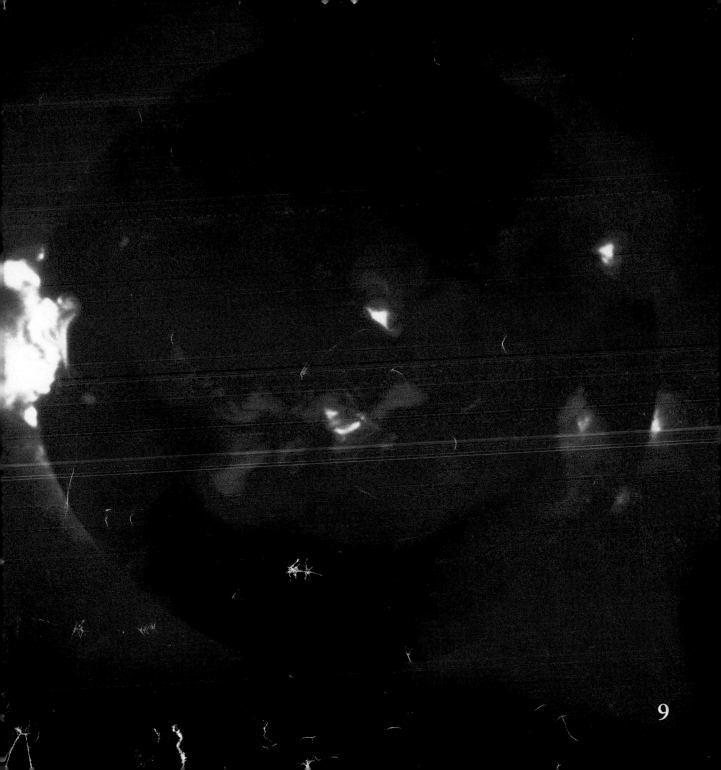

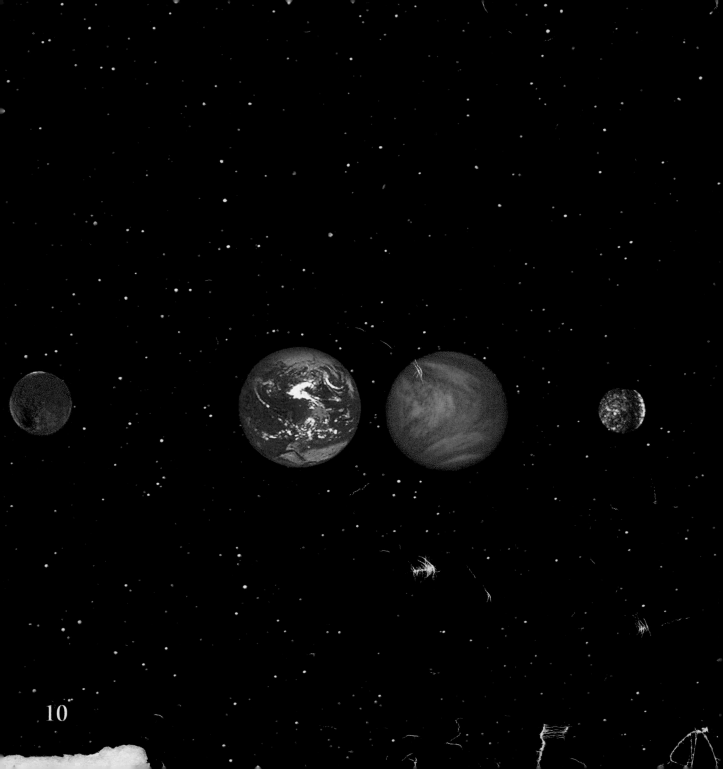

THE INNER PLANETS

The four planets closest to the Sun—Mercury, Venus, Earth, and Mars—are little worlds of rock. Three of them—all but Mercury—are wrapped in a cocoon of air. Today we know a lot about these planets. So let's visit each of them, including our own.

The four inner planets are airless Mercury, cloudy Venus, watery Earth, and dusty Mars. Here they are compared in size to the much larger Sun.

Mercury

Early in the life of the Solar System all of the planets were pelted with space bombs of rock, metal, and ice called *planetesimals*. Each explosion blasted out a crater. In 1974 the spacecraft *Mariner 10* flew to Mercury and sent back pictures showing that Mercury is scarred by thousands of craters. Because Mercury has hardly any air and no water to wear away the rock, the planet's craters look as fresh today as when they were made more than four billion years ago.

Mercury is the most heavily cratered object in the Solar System. It also has many high cliffs, probably formed when the young planet cooled and its rocky crust wrinkled.

13

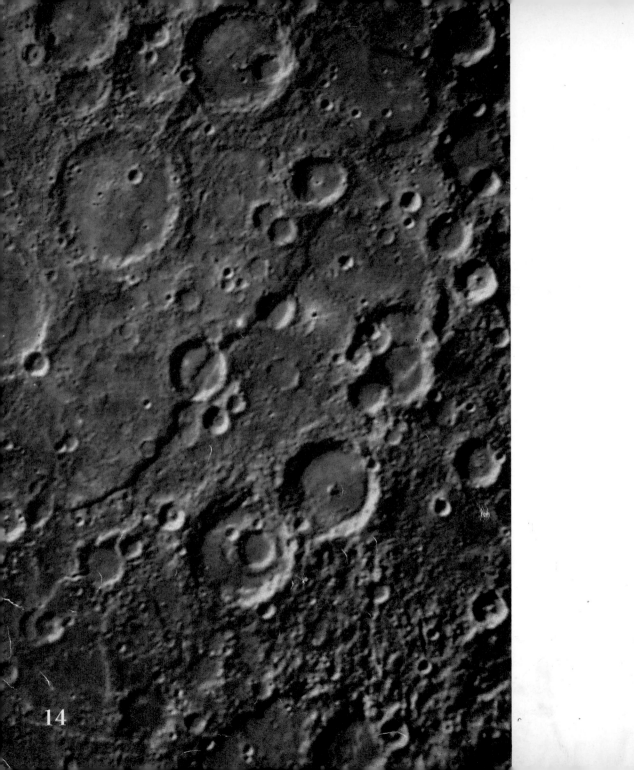

14

A climb across Mercury's surface would be not only difficult but very painful. Mercury is so close to the Sun that it heats up to more than 600° Fahrenheit (330° Celsius). That's hot enough to melt lead. And because Mercury has hardly a breath of air to trap this heat, the temperature at night plunges to -290°F (-180°C).

Mercury's many craters were formed billions of years ago after its crust became solid. Thousands of objects also crashed into Mercury's surface, leaving circular dents.

Venus

The second planet is forever hidden beneath a thick cover of clouds. Its air is poisonous to breathe and so thick that walking on the planet would be like wading against a gentle river current. Venus's heavy blanket of air also makes the sky red instead of blue, because blue light is blocked by the dense air. The air also acts as a heat trap that keeps the planet's surface a blazing 880°F (470°C). That's hot enough to make the rocks glow.

Venus's thick clouds of sulfuric acid and carbon dioxide hide the planet's surface from view and act as a heat trap.

17

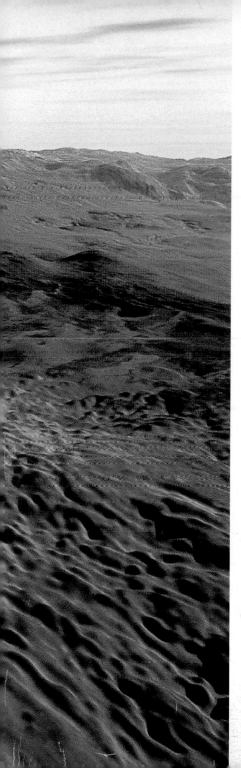

Venus's sky is lit up by a never-ending lightning storm. As each bolt flashes, the roar of thunder echoes off the planet's mountains and across its many inactive volcanoes. Much of Venus seems to be covered with lava from ancient volcano eruptions.

Radar images made by the Magellan *spacecraft gave us this view of Venus's large volcano Sapas Mons.*

Earth

Earth is the only planet with liquid water. It is also the only planet with a "friendly" *atmosphere*, or air, that we can breathe. Earth's air is mostly nitrogen with a smaller amount of oxygen, the gas that keeps us alive. Our atmosphere serves as a blanket that keeps the planet warm at night. People, elephants, seals, and spiders couldn't live on any other planet.

Earth is made mostly of rock. But its center is a huge ball of the metals iron and nickel. Millions of years ago a large planetesimal smashed into Earth and sliced off a chunk of rock that became the Moon.

Did you know that right now you are racing along at more than 67,000 miles (108,000 kilometers) an hour? That is Earth's average speed as it travels around the Sun every 365¼ days.

You can see all of Africa on this satellite image of Earth. The tan regions are desert. Forests appear green. The white patches are clouds.

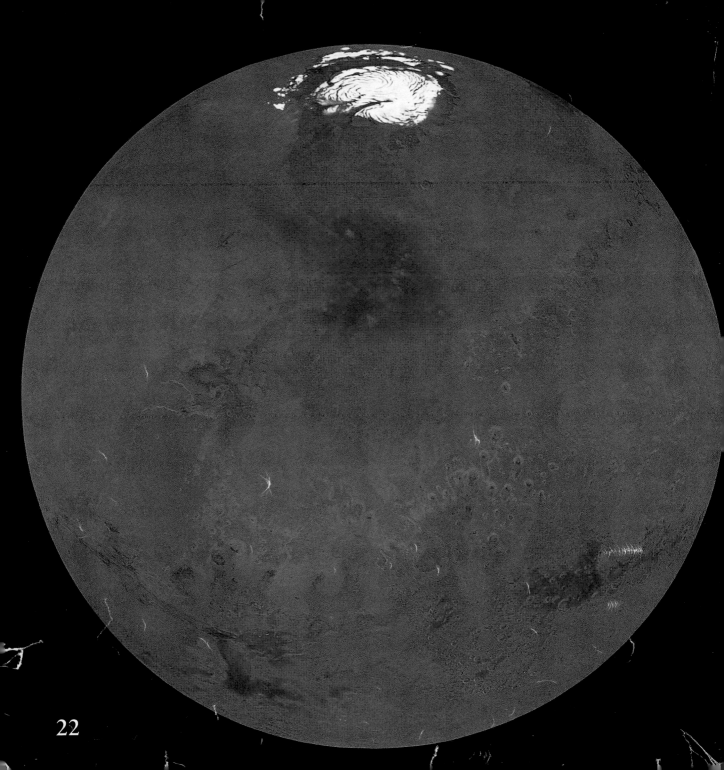

22

Mars

If you're a mountain climber, you'll love Mars. It has the largest known mountain in the entire Solar System, Olympus Mons. This giant towers more than three times higher than Earth's tallest mountain, Mount Everest. Plunked down in the middle of Texas, Olympus Mons would cover almost half the state.

Mars is a dry world a bit smaller than Earth. The north polar cap, a thin sheet of carbon dioxide ice, shines brightly at the top.

A broad and deep valley carved into Mars is named Valles Marineris. It is more than ten times longer than Earth's Grand Canyon and four times as deep. Also called the Red Planet, Mars gets its reddish color from rusty rocks. Mars has an atmosphere, but the air is too thin to be of use to you. Without a special space suit, you wouldn't be able to breathe, because the Martian air is made of carbon dioxide, not oxygen.

In 1997, the space probe Sojourner *rolled up for a closer look at a Martian rock named Yogi. Controlled by workers back on Earth, little* Sojourner *was sent to study these foreign rocks.*

THE GAS GIANTS

Four of the five outer planets are gas giants—Jupiter, Saturn, Uranus, and Neptune. They are enormous globes of colorful gases with balls of rock tucked in the center. What would a visit to these planets be like?

Here, we can see the four gas giants—Jupiter, Saturn, Uranus, and Neptune—compared in size to the Sun.

27

Jupiter

King of the planets, Jupiter is one and a half times bigger than all the other planets put together. Thirteen hundred Earths could fit inside this huge gas giant. By the latest count, the planet has sixteen moons. Its air appears as colorful bands of mostly hydrogen. An enormous rusty-red feature larger than Earth floats in Jupiter's upper atmosphere. Called the Great Red Spot, it is probably a storm system that has been raging for more than three hundred years.

Jupiter (top left) with its four largest moons—Callisto (lower left), then Ganymede, Europa, and Io. Some of Jupiter's twelve more moons are most likely asteroids captured by the planet's powerful gravity.

To visit Jupiter and its moons, you'd need to float above it in a balloon because there is no ground to land on. Its upper layers of gases are hundreds of degrees below zero. But deep down, things start to heat up. There, the gases probably turn to hydrogen slush. Even farther down the hydrogen becomes as hard as cement. At the planet's center there may be a rock and ice core about the size of Earth.

Io is Jupiter's closest and most colorful moon. The darker areas are volcanoes, which pour out lava. An astronomer once said Io reminds him of a pizza.

31

The ringed planet, Saturn, with the spacecraft Voyager 1 floating above. Like Jupiter, Saturn's cold atmosphere is mostly hydrogen.

Saturn

The "planet with ears"—that's what the astronomer Galileo called Saturn when he first saw it through his telescope in the year 1610. The "ears" turned out to be the fuzzy edges of Saturn's beautiful system of rings, which Galileo could not see clearly.

Like Jupiter, Saturn has a striped atmosphere of mostly hydrogen along with clouds of ammonia snow. Winds eleven times stronger than a hurricane tear at these clouds, whose temperatures are as low as -180°F (-118°C). Also like Jupiter, Saturn has no surface to walk on. Deep inside its gases heat up, and the high pressure turns them to slush.

What would a trip through the planet's rings be like? The rings are made of lumps of dirty ice. Some are as small as a golf ball. Others are as large as a train car. These frozen chunks may be matter left over from the time the planets formed. Or they may be broken pieces of an ancient moon that wandered too close to the planet and was torn apart by Saturn's strong gravity.

Thousands of smaller ringlets make up Saturn's ring system. When packed together, all of this icy matter would make a giant snowball 60 miles (100 kilometers) wide.

Uranus

The third gas giant, Uranus, is four times bigger than Earth. It is a tilted world, with its poles pointing sideways instead of up and down. The gas methane in the planet's upper atmosphere gives Uranus a pale greenish glow. The planet has rings and twenty known moons. If you plunged through the planet's freezing cold air, you would probably splash into a deep sea of scalding ammonia and water. Uranus may have a core of rock and ice about the size of Earth.

While the other planets spin like tops, Uranus is a planet tilted on its side. It appears to roll around the Sun in its orbit.

Neptune

With its pale blue hydrogen cloud cover, Neptune is the last of the four gas giants. It is a sister planet of Uranus, with its freezing upper atmosphere that heats up closer to its core. Its center may be a burning slush ball of liquid water, ammonia, and methane. While Jupiter has its Great Red Spot, Neptune has a Great Dark Spot, which also seems to be a storm that has been raging for centuries. When the *Voyager* spacecraft sped over Neptune's north pole in the 1980s at 61,000 miles (98,170 kilometers) an hour, it counted eight moons. It also photographed rings made of dust and ice chips.

A view of Neptune rising above its inner moon, Triton. From time to time, jets of liquid nitrogen spurt through the weak spots in Triton's crust.

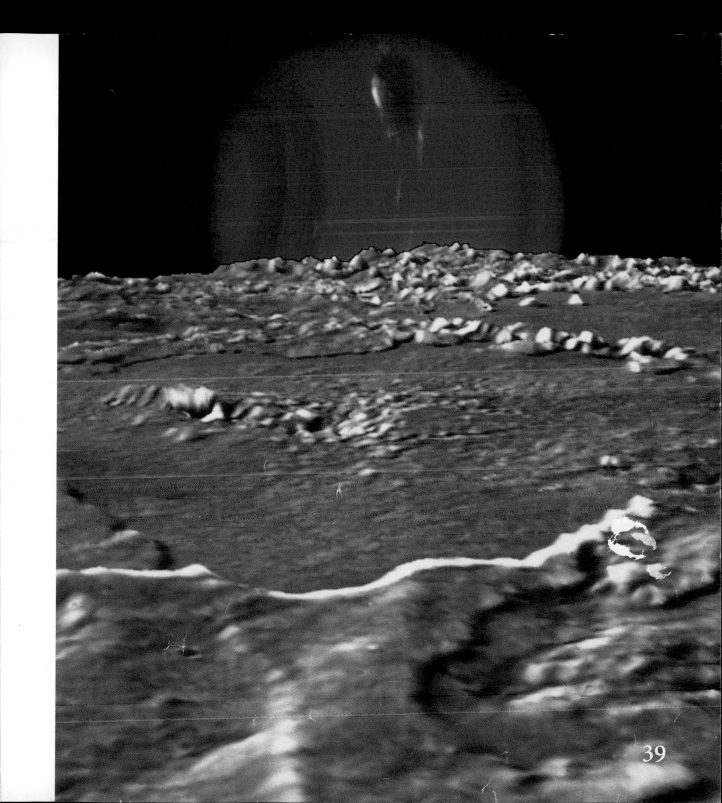

39

Pluto is the midget of the Solar System. Here, we see Pluto from its moon, Charon, with the distant Sun in the background.

A PLANET IN DISGUISE

Finally we reach Pluto, the last planet to be discovered and the one that is a bit of a mystery.

Pluto

Pluto is the farthest planet in the Solar System. Its great distance makes Pluto and its one moon, Charon, hard to study. Pluto is a tiny world made up mostly of nitrogen and methane ice that reach temperatures as low as -400°F (-240°C).

Although oddball Pluto is officially a planet, many astronomers think of it as a fake. It seems to be a big chunk of ice that was flung out of a large swarm of icy objects lying far beyond Neptune's orbit. The iceball, along with its snowball of a moon, then settled into an orbit around the Sun. Pluto is the slowpoke of the Solar System, taking 248 Earth years to circle the Sun.

ACROSS THE BORDER

We've slid along Saturn's rings, climbed the mountains of Mars, and sizzled on the surface of Venus. But mostly we've seen how the Solar System stretches out so far that it is mostly empty space.

And now that we're back home, Earth seems like the perfect place to live. One thing our tour has shown us is that only Earth has the right atmosphere to support all its living things.

Are there other Solar Systems out there in the darkness of space? Only recently have we been able to answer yes to that question. So far, astronomers have discovered more than a dozen stars that have one or more planets orbiting them. In the years ahead, they will most likely discover many more.

As this Voyager space probe leaves the Solar System and enters deep space,
it is carrying recorded messages. Perhaps someday intelligent life-forms
will listen to these messages from Earth and know they are not alone.

GLOSSARY

Astronomer   A scientist who studies all known objects in the Universe, how they are arranged, what they are made of, and how they move.

Atmosphere   The air around a planet.

Fixed Star   A term used in ancient times to describe the stars. The stars were seen to move as a group across the sky. For that reason, they were said to be "fixed" in place.

Gravity   The force that causes any two objects in the Universe to attract each other. It is also the force that keeps you firmly on Earth rather than being flung off into space by Earth's spinning.

Orbit   The path a planet follows as it circles its local star.

Planet   An object such as Earth, Jupiter, or Mars that orbits about a star.

Planetesimals   Icy, rocky, and metallic pieces of matter that formed early in the life of the Solar System and that collected into those objects we call planets.

Solar System   Our home planetary system consisting of nine known planets, more than sixty moons, millions of asteroids, and millions of comets.

Wandering Star   A term from ancient times for a planet.

FIND OUT MORE

Books

Bendrick, Jeanne. *Moons and Rings: Companions to the Planets.* Brookfield, CT: Milbrook, 1991.

——. *The Planets: Neighbors in Space.* Brookfield, CT: Millbrook, 1991.

Berger, Melvin. *Looking at the Planets: A Book about the Solar System.* New York: Scholastic, 1995.

Branley, Franklyn M. *The Planets in Our Solar System.* New York: HarperCollins, 1998.

Burrows, William E. *Mission to Deep Space: Voyager's Interplanetary Odyssey.* New York: W H Freeman, 1993.

Dickinson, Terence. *Other Worlds: A Beginner's Guide to Planets and Moons.* Buffalo, NY: Firefly, 1995.

Estalella, Robert. *Planets and Satellites.* Hauppauge, NY: Barron, 1992.

Gibbons, Gail. *The Planets.* New York: Holiday House, 1994.

Lauber, Patricia. *Journey to the Planets.* New York: Crown, 1990.

Milton, Jacqueline. *Discovering the Planets.* Mahwah, NJ: Troll, 1991.

Murray, Peter. *The Planets.* Chanhassen, MN: Child's World, 1992.

Simon, Seymour. *Our Solar System.* New York: Morrow, 1992.

Sims, Lesley. *The Planets.* Austin: Raintree Steck-Vaugh, 1994.

Websites

The Nine Planets
seds.lpl.arizona.edu/billa/tnp/nineplanets.html

Solar System Simulator
space.jpl.nasa.gov

Planetary Globes You Can Make
www.hawastsoc.org/solar/eng/ico.html

The Planetary System Electronic Picturebook
www.stsci.edu/exined/Planetary.html

Volcanoes of the Solar System Electronic Picturebook
www.stsci.edu/exined/Volcanic.html

Amazing Space/Solar System Trading Cards
opposite.stsci.edu/pubinfo/education/amazing-space/trading-top-level.html

Welcome to the Planets
pds.jpl.nasa.gov/planets/welcome.html

AUTHOR'S BIO

Roy A. Gallant, called "one of the deans of American science writers for children" by *School Library Journal*, is the author of more than eighty books on scientific subjects. Since 1979, he has been director of the Southworth Planetarium at the University of Southern Maine, where he holds an adjunct full professorship. He lives in Rangeley, Maine.

INDEX